TEKIAH

Tekiah

poems by

Richard Chess

 University of Tampa Press • Tampa, Florida • 2002

Copyright © 1994 by Richard Chess
Cover photograph copyright © 2002 by Richard Chess
All rights reserved

New Edition

ISBN 1-879852-78-0 (pbk)

The Yemenite shofar reproduced on the cover is approximately three feet in length. It was presented to the author in celebration of the first edition of *Tekiah*.

Cover design by Ana Montalvo.
Designed and typeset in Centaur and Janson types by Richard Mathews

Manufactured in the United States of America
Printed on acid-free paper

University of Tampa Press
401 West Kennedy Blvd.
Tampa, FL 33606

Browse & order online at
http://utpress.ut.edu

Library of Congress Control Number: 2002108683

The Library of Congress has cataloged the first edition as follows:

Library of Congress Cataloging in Publication Data

Chess, Richard.

Tekiah: poems / by Richard Chess.
   p. cm.
   ISBN 0-8203-1678-4 (pbk.: alk. Paper)
   I. Jews—United States—Poetry. I. Title.

ps3553.H42T45   1994
811'.54—dc20   94-9199

To My Mother and Father

And it shall come to pass . . .
that a great horn shall be blown;
and they shall come that were
lost in the land of Assyria.

–Isaiah 27:13

Contents

Baby Boomer   1

Growing Up in a Jewish Neighborhood   2

"With the Blast of the Ram's Horn"   4

Trip to the Museum   5

The Wrestler   7

That's How It Is   8

The Good Jew   10

Ofra Haza   12

Guardians   14

Prayer for the Bride   16

The Skin That Shelters   18

The End of the Retreat   19

Nothing but Pleasure   21

Notes from a Jewish Suburb   22

The Drunk Rabbi   24

The Rabbi Masturbates   25

The Rabbi's Tongue   27

New Song   28

Lovers of *Torah*   29

Rock and Redeemer   30

The Rabbi Disturbed   32

Rabbi *qua* Mystic   33

God   35

Father   36

The Rabbi's Hand   37

At the Rabbi's Study Group   39

The Week   40

From the Introduction to the New Revised Prayer Book   41

Harvest Booth   42

The Tenth Emanation of Creation   43

The Rest of the Year   44

Survivors   46

Yiddish Poets in America   47

Holocaust Day   48

The Rabbi's Wife   49

My People   50

The Jewish Angel   51

Rabbi in the Garden   52

The Rabbi Who Does Not Observe   53

The Eve of *Rosh Hashanah*, 500 Years after the Inquisition   54

After the Ritual Purification   56

Noah's Death Mask   58

David's Body   59

Tzimtzum: Contraction   60

The Knot   62

Witnesses   63

Making Cain   64

Bless Us with Peace, Angels of Peace   65

The Rabbi's Sabbatical   66

Two and One   67

Tekiah Gedolah   68

TEKIAH

Baby Boomer

The couple in their giddy bed rose
and collapsed, rose and collapsed
until a flash, a gay explosion,
and she was pregnant and he stood
framed in the rectangular winter light.

Whose fruitful thought was it that they multiply?
Some fatherly absence disturbed them,
and the rivers and fields salted with bodies.

Now he smoked, and she grew indelicately fat.
Like German soldiers defeated
by this conception, minutes fell from the clock.
The window was singed with frost.

My parents parted then,
but heaven had already been
severed from earth
so I felt nothing in the womb,
that dank Jewish museum.

Growing Up in a Jewish Neighborhood

He wants to go
Where no one freezes
When the phone rings

When meat is sliced, he wants
The stench of blood
To concentrate his hunger

Once he saw
His grandmother's breasts
They were sour yellow stars

He wants a crow
That speaks not Yiddish
But its own ugly language

The seasons enclose him
Like a barbed-wire fence
His name is a button

Stitched to a coat
A style his grandfather in Minsk
Might have worn

At the urinal
Connie Mack Stadium
He wants his penis to signify

Nothing
He wants to reach for the stone
Flashing in the river

Without thinking
Of Aunt Dora
He wants the glass of a broken window

To tell no story
He wants an empty pocket
He wants new shoes

"With the Blast of the Ram's Horn"

The Hebrew teacher, Mrs. Melnick, read
A verse aloud. Her hair in careless knots,
Her acned face—worse when she'd smile
At us, those nasty blossoms on her cheeks.

A battered map of Israel on the board
Reminded us, as she reminded us,
We were too poor in spirit for Jerusalem,
Spelled without vowels, of course, in Hebrew.

We craved the milk and meat of life:
Baseball before dark closed
The baseball field forever. Whack!
A ruler brought us back to Melnick.

No light to dream in left, we prayed.
At 6:15 the bell, the parking lot
Of parents aggravated by their jobs,
The storm of our dispersion.

Trip to the Museum

In the glass case we see a star
Torn from the shoulder of a mother's coat
And the spoon with which she fed her child soup.
If in the glass you see a grave reflection,
Don't be alarmed, children, don't be ashamed.
That face you must learn to love.
Let's move on now, another class is near.

Here's a picture of a wagon, piled high with bread
To last a week, here Bazarny Square
Where furniture is sold for fuel.
Imagine breaking up your living room for heat.

In this next shot, before she boards the train
A woman kneels to write a farewell letter.
A crowd surrounds her.
Beyond the frame, guards
Fire to speed the day along.

Look closely now. The hill you see—shoes.
It would take days, years to hear the stories
Each sole could tell of dancing at a ghetto
Wedding or plodding winter streets
Where bodies lay
Or breathing when removed from a woman
Shuffled into the shower—Oh,
Forgive me, I come here once a year
To dream, not quite
To dream, to stir the ashes of my own . . .

I wear a modest skirt, you see, and speak
In muted tones. I choose the spring to lead this trip,
A fragrant week of orchids:
When we enter and depart
Our tongues are tipped with sweetness.
Who can remember the taste of your own birth?

It's time to picnic. Fling
Yourselves—history
Is done-into the sun.

The Wrestler

When that stinking angel Ed, the smartest boy
      in violet shorts, lifted and dropped
me to the mat, when that slob landed
      on me, I went deaf to the skinny birds
who ringed the mat with jeers,
      heard only my breath escaping.
For a dizzy moment I mistook him
      for one of the dumbbell-tough thugs
who flicks ashes at girlish boys,
      but then I flipped onto my safe belly
and rose, ass first, to shake this nuisance
      from my back.
He dropped me by the thighs this time
      and worked my shoulder blades
to the floor. No prayer could save me.
      On the count of three Ed rose
like vapor and vanished down a dark corridor
      toward some book, no doubt,
leaving me, the blessed son of Isaac,
      crushed on the matted earth
from which my children have risen
      to take revenge.

That's How It Is

Brooklyn, 1963

Your mother over the house
like a Chagall bride.
A few rungs below the moon.
Married to nothing human, she sings
a kind of anti-lullaby.
Angels also traffic that ladder, some
like lightbulbs excited with messages
they descend to deliver,
others, their filaments spent, return
with dim expressions.
And though the night's amply disturbed
with the chattering of wings, her voice
alone keeps you up.
As far as you know, that's how it is
between mothers and daughters,
with a story she tucks you in,
with a kiss closes your eyes,
then before you can sink
into the warm sand of sleep,
she has turned into a winged nightmare
with the voice of a crow
come for the gifts she has given you.
What is it tonight?
The necklace with the black stone,
the jewelry box into which it is folded,
the drawer in which the box sleeps like a tourist,
the bureau itself, that outbound ocean liner?
Perhaps tonight she'll seize

the whole room, the space
that tricks you into believing the world
a navigable, generous place.
It's late, very late
when you cry *father*, who is not
a happy groom. In fact, he is
hardly a man at all anymore,
fifteen years with your mother,
carrying the stringless violin
she gave him, stuttering like
a goat when she permits him
to speak.

The Good Jew

No one suspects a Jew among the hogs,
so we buckle into overalls and a dialect
that rings true in the muddy pen.
We pet the heavy skulls

with a soft hand, we feed
the intelligent beasts
choice grain, we hum a little Bach
to our civilized friends, then turn

a neat profit from the pink meat
packaged with a halo of pineapple.
By five the Yiddish intonation like a shadow
to the face returns, so we retreat and pray

for rain if the land needs rain:
we have a certain claim on God
and could request a flood of miracles
should we be so moved.

Later, shaved and dressed in tweed,
by candlelight we dine, sensibly, cheap,
by candlelight review our master plan
in which, of course, you have a part.

I tell you this in confidence,
for should some other Jew,
less favorably disposed to Gentiles,
learn of my betrayal,

he could call at once
the loans on which you live,
from me, recall this voice.

Ofra Haza

A young Israeli singer
Whose family ascended from Yemen
On the legendary flight

That goes like this: a plane lands
And it doesn't take the village Jews
A minute to figure out what's coming down:

The great prophesied bird
To redeem them. It's 1949, the end
Of days! They climb inside

The belly, build a small
Fire in the aisle to roast a feast!
What music they make,

Flaring inside an El Al beat.
How the flustered crew
Flurries to douse it!

Home on the longed-for ground,
They banish these primitives
To border towns,

But her voice cannot be bound,
It sears desert and city,
It sizzles on every track.

I taped *50 Gates of Wisdom* from a CD,
A fire blown from machine to machine.
I'm no fool. I love henna

And a Yemenite woman who seasons
Music with a dozen
Dissonant spices.

Guardians

Variations on a Theme from Psalm 34

1

The Lord's angel guards
those who revere Him, and rescues them.

2

Everyone knows you
are accompanied by an angel
who dresses in silk, douses herself in perfume,
and thirsts like Sappho or Rimbaud
    for the milky breast.
You are accompanied by flamboyance herself!

3

She studies your books, the Lord's angel, your music
    note by note.
Now she has a thought that will occur to you
in, perhaps, twenty years.

4

A stranger in the garden, the moon
excites the angel.

Let us dance, she says,
And slips into wings and lifts
Her skirt from the ground.

5

At dawn you hear
whimpering in the garden:
the cry of an animal only different,
the song of a sick rose.

It is the Lord's angel suffering there, it is your life.
Go, rescue it.

Prayer for the Bride

The azalea flames honor you,
With the chatter of wings, butterflies
Paired like sisters honor you.
Oak leaves quaver like telegrams
From the living and dead.
The day gathers sherds of a ceremonial plate
To form a brilliant, white betrothal sun,
And the moon, with its slow gallop,
The tumbleweed stars—
In your honor the wedding-night sky resounds!

When like our ancestors we go forth to wander the earth,
When we fall the way they have fallen,
May the braided light that rises from the wedding canopy
Be there, a thousand miles or more from the temple,
To lift us.
If the rose of infidelity should blossom
Or a child be twisted from our care
By whatever wind would claim it,
If disease or boredom or despair
Should carve its name into our heart,
May the light repair the sky torn by our cry.

Take the hand of my loneliness.
Today let us leave behind bruised fruit.
Wear the antique dress and I will wear the robe
Which one day will be my shroud.
To a feast of the highest order, come,
To Jerusalem we will fly,

Not the city of goat light, city of scars,
But the capital that crowns the steep slope of the sea.
What light will come upon us then I cannot say,
Having been there only once, before birth.
Let us begin to build a life
Here, where the road ends
At a surge of mountain, lift and shine!

The Skin That Shelters

The marriage feast dwindled to fire.
Like bushes against flame, cousins
Or sisters featureless figured the dark.
Still, the stars seemed to point toward my bride.

But I was no seer.
In tent-light, my woolly hands
Drew back a blanket, uncovering my reward.
Rachel's sheepish body quivered at my touch;
Her breath darted at my flesh.
I drank from the perfumed well where I'd spied her
Seven years ago with her father's flock.

I might have dreamed that night, I don't recall;
The skin that sheltered us
Was bloodstained at dawn.
No band of goats besieged the desert silence:
Had my brother ravaged Laban's camp?
Leah lay beside me, wise with deceit.

The End of the Retreat

You wore a smock smeared indigo, a chalky
layer of which tinted your good legs and zinc-colored hair.

It gave you an eerie industrial look, as if you were blown
into the shape of a human

by the abstract pastel wind of your work.
Even away from work, you seem somewhere between.

The day we swam to the dam, I raced ahead.
When I looked back I saw a thin smile

on the lake's surface and spiraling smoke of hair.
When I called out, you said school mornings

mother, just home from waitressing,
was like a guard

at the gate between two worlds:
at the kitchen table she waited to kiss you

home from dreams and off to class.
Maybe when you've had a decent childhood,

as an adult you're able to swim
in two lakes at once. I don't know.

I'm married, one of the reasons I couldn't
love you, couldn't orgasm

then roll back to see
what's been done—that's history—

and try to figure out
where the cry of red

came from after years working blue—that's therapy.
I didn't break

a plate—not when I said goodbye.
The only tangible thing

I inherited from my mother was one china plate.
In honor of her, I broke it

at my betrothal.
Even at a joyous occasion, we recall

the Temple, Chmielnicki, Warsaw—the whole
damned litany.

And trust, you can smash it as gleefully as you can
a plate—it takes a master to piece it back together,

or magic, which we mostly lack. So I wound down
the gravel driveway from your studio, tires grinding sherds

into the dirt, and alone I drove
Route 29, my wife in the empty seat beside me,

your pastels in front of me, a cerulean curtain
I had to part to see.

Nothing but Pleasure

Do you know the history of light?
First God created man and woman,
and in the darkness they were one.
Their lives nothing but pleasure.
His hand moved over her form
like breath over water, her hand
moved like music through air.
But there was no music, no cello,
no flute, only the uplifted
cup of silence from which they drank.
Only when one of them, wobbly
with joy, pricked the air with speech,
only when he began to name what he felt
when kissed or when her palm
anchored on his belly,
only when he learned to distinguish
this pleasure from that, did the light come,
the light in which differences—in shape,
value, song—shone, the light
their children and children's children
tried to change or extinguish or ignore,
coupling with eyes closed, composing
a fugue of the amplified dark.

Notes from a Jewish Suburb

Work

Oaks haggle with the wind
Over the price of winter.
Otherwise, business is slow,
Sunlight and shadows
The only traffic
Through the showroom.

Marriage

Should be—muddy
Regret, sharp tooth
And claw—left
Outside, but
Can't return
Without tracking
Something across
The waxed floor.

Dreams

Broadcast like the late-night news,
Volume up throughout the neighborhood
Awash in gold.

And he who works late
Lets his people sleep.

Grief

Grief of the chair
When the sitter leans back.
Then there's commercial grief
For which an over-the-counter cure
Is available. But nothing cures
A parent's grief: she's outlived
Her usefulness.

Prayer

Gathers in a chapel.
Few notice the lights burning there.
Not that they would
Extinguish the lights, mindful of waste.
They'll pay almost anything to keep
The lights, a few old men, burning there.

The Drunk Rabbi

At the table, the rabbi
Entertains the law, his brow blazing, Sinai at twilight.
Under the watch of his wise men, his good students,
   he slips
Over the border of his sovereignty.
Though now forbidden to heed
His decree, three schnapps
They wait for him to rule.
Exuberance, he says, *springs*
From the heart and should
Be expressed freely.
Though we wrap ourselves in laws
As in the finest leather,
We must not live bound
To life. He lifts a jigger.
At the mention of the *malakh hamavet*, the angel
Who spirits the soul away from the body,
His followers sing to shield themselves
And disperse down sober paths.
Alone, their rabbi sways as if entranced
By a dancer who breathes on his neck.
The schnapps gone, the hour late, the Kingdom
Beckons through an open gate.

The Rabbi Masturbates

A fly screams
Past the ear   Damned

Nuisance or demon
Here for the furious

Motion of his hand
Laughter rips the sky

Lilith appears
Her skirt a cataract

Her drum the tambour
His semen leaps

And scatters
She regards him

With an eye of moon
And an eye of iron

His pants deflated
His sex untuned

The seeds ascend
Neither the narrow

Feminine passage
Nor the sky-ladder

Her wings flap
He wipes his mess

And walks away
Barefoot on the moss

The Rabbi's Tongue

At rest it lies
In the mouth guarded
By two walls bone

And flesh   Awake
It springs the board
From which   clothed in phonemes

The soul dives
Into the world
And swims like a rumor

From one ear
To another
A sugar cube dissolves

On the rabbi's tongue
It beckons you
With *keep this*

Between us It curls

New Song

Played on timbrel and lyre,
Jew's harp and synthesizer,
On wood and skin, carillon and chimes,
Zither and mandolin.

Played at morning and night,
For animals and men,
To mark a beginning, measure an end,
By a lake and in the lobby of a grand hotel,
To praise heaven, blast hell.

The priest plays his song
But never for the dead, blemished, maimed or scarred.
He plays from the heights,
And the melody bounds forth,
The notes pour as from a decanter
Into a fragile glass.

Played on cymbal and kazoo.
The priest plays his, we play ours in a bar.
On the comb, the saw, the calliope,
We play to raise the dead.
He plays to purify the soul,
We play to keep it whole,
Shadow and light, night and day,
On the river and porch,
Amongst a crowd and alone,
On the spoon and bassoon, in tails and jeans,
On the timbrel and lyre,
Jew's harp, synthesizer.

Lovers of *Torah*

A seductress, *Torah*
Lifts its veil for the swift
Eye, fixes its gaze
On a gentleman in the corner
Surrender surrender she commands
Enchanted by her belly
And jewels, he obeys

   *

Handsomely attired, sure
In speech, she lends delight
At evening's end, candles
Snuffed, goblets shelved
To the guest who lingers
The *Torah* offers
A portion of her wealth
She stands proudly
Her riches displayed

   *

Scorned ignored
Badgered burned caressed
Raped   She is ours
We are Hers
Bound flayed released
We fly

Rock and Redeemer

God was with me once
His big eye staring
Out from the wound I licked

My lover's and His
Labored breathing
A mistake

Inviting Him
To save me
I tried to

Sleep I ducked
Under a barricade
Marched in a parade

Your big eye
Your heavy
Breathing Your fat lips

Parted, about to speak
I had made a mistake
Losing myself

In prayer I liked
The rise
And dip the power

Of a hundred
Voices singing
Spiritedly

Nothing could be purer
Unbuttoning a blouse
Bowing to

The scroll God was
With me His big
Eye heavy

Breathing fat lips
His absolute
Refusal to budge

The Rabbi Disturbed

Has death alighted
On your shoulder flapped
Its wings and flown

Before you could
Trap it This afternoon
You slide from room

To room as if
Seeking a shoe
Glasses a phone

Number You extend
A hand to the table
A glass of milk

But your shoulder
Too sore to lift it
The bell rings

A eulogy at the door
Greets you by your good name
Its long hair sweeps

The ground It reaches
For you its arm a branch
On which you could rest

Rabbi *qua* Mystic

He dabbles
In the occult His body

He listens to it
Swell subside

He practices automatic
Writing He submits

To a colony of bees He keeps
Major and minor fasts

He regards his son
He chants

Torah from last to first
To close the circle

He drinks his wife
He returns

His tongue to the talking stones
Fingers to the fronds

Blood to the fountain
He assembles

Sherds of a broken vessel
Alphabet of a lost

Language he arranges
And rearranges

The letters to hold
Light to form

Unutterable names
He cleaves

Like an infant to
Our mother's sore breast

God

She receives us in the garden
To stroll and enjoy the fragrances.
She prizes tomatoes and roses and praises
Her gardener and assures us
She loves company.
Why, then, we wonder, does she live
Here, so far from town, an estate
Spacious enough to wander
For days, months even, without
Human contact. She anticipates our needs,
Serves mint tea an instant
Before we thirst, inquires
Of our health as a cancer,
Undiagnosed, crawls up my colon.
We know not to ask
Of her family—what losses, what
Disappointments she must have suffered—
But cannot shake the queer feeling
That if we were shown the room
Where family photos hang
We'd find ourselves there.
We tire before she tires.
She invites us to spend the night.
Such beautiful hair, ageless eyes—
We must be mad to decline.

Father

My soul, my three-part soul,
        Laborer, idler, smooth talker;

My lower, middle and upper souls;
My window-shopping soul, my tranquil soul,
        My hitchhiking soul;

My soul that seeks its father.

My soul travels between stations
        Of mercy and power, beauty and endurance,
And waits on the platform for the next train.

What do the Kabbalists know about my soul?
        He walked away long ago.

My simple soul on the platform
        Till the next train.

The Rabbi's Hand

It has squeezed
A baseball   It has read
An engraved

Stone Prague cemetery
It has been read by an occultist
It has torn orchid

Petals wings
Of a butterfly letters
From the woman whose body

It trusted   It has struck
Matches searched the pockets
Of a friend's coat while he slept

It has opened and closed
Around a thought   It has trimmed
A penis and wrapped

The foreskin in cloth
It has crushed roaches
It has fingered the Torah

With a silver touch
It has been immersed in ice
It has opened millions of doors

It has pointed to stars
It has been a language
Two travelers invented

It has five fingers
It is amoral   It is warm

At the Rabbi's Study Group

When the room is like a cup
Just before wine is poured into it,
He asks. How could those men,
After the temple, kicking through rubble,
Not have suffered, amidst grief, a little boredom?
What else could account for
Their concentration on slight matters:
Must one recite the morning prayer
Before the light turns from blue
To green, or blue to white;
Will the echo of a ram's horn suffice
To remind men of the near sacrifice.
Aren't we, half awake, as one
Wandering by the cave of a text
Anxious to hear the echo
Of a voice long ago expired?
The rituals of this time, this place,
Aren't they intended to propel us
Deeper into boredom
Where God might be
Picking His scabs?
Only the rabbi's wife is disturbed
By this nonsense. She hisses and spits
Like a beast defending its nest.
The others, including the rabbi himself,
Have drifted. In the distance, a siren
Scales the darkness, beds everywhere
Take on water, soon to sink.

The Week

Now in its sixth day, like a pear it has sweetened
nearly beyond belief.
Already this week he has blessed a bread
baked by a man whose testicles have been eaten by cancer,
already he has heard a Bat Mitzvah student
sing Isaiah like an angel
waiting outside his study door.
This morning he pulls the blue shirt
from the closet and now, *tefillin*
snaked around his arm, begins to sway.
Does he pray for the brick by brick
rebuilding of the Temple,
or for the hour when children to their parents
will turn like tiger to lamb,
or for his wife, eating her egg?
In a few hours she will arrive at the clinic, quietly
cross the sacred line
picketers make, and sign in for the abortion.
She scours the pan
to a reflecting finish, hesitates
at the still sink, and notices
through the window a cardinal in the yard.
Upstairs he sings, a rabbi out of key,
carried away on a skin of light, shaking
his free hand at the sun.

From the Introduction to the New Revised Prayer Book

If you pray, skip to the end.

In a room without prayer, be a prayer.
Without a chair, be a chair.
With a pencil, erase.

Face any window: wall, grief, lamp.

The Baal Shem Tov: *Imagine a man whose business hounds him through many streets and across the marketplace the livelong day.*

Say *she* when the prayer reads *he*.
Say *dust* when the prayer reads *dust*.

Shekinah,
King of Kings,
Ayn Sof.

Some meaningless prayers, repeated
until meaningless, a needle
sewing with no eye.

Forget the prayers. Spend the day
not talking to bark.

Mendel of Kotzk: *A woodcutter, who spends most of the day sharpening the saw and only the last hour cutting the wood, has earned his day's wages.*

Give away your house before you pray.

Give away the prayer.

Harvest Booth

He shakes *lulav* and *etrog*
In the four directions,
Toward the source of song
And speech, heart and brain.

He invokes ancestors
To join them in the annual booth.
He summons the stars
Through the bamboo roof.

His wife like myrtle and willow
And branches of palm
Shakes, shakes in her yellow
Dress as she recites a psalm.

Though plentifully blessed, still
They inquire of their guests,
Will this year bring a child?
Father Abraham sighs, Mother Ruth directs

Their gaze away from her.
They sip wine, chew bread,
Living, dead, unborn together,
A harvest in a holiday bed.

The Tenth Emanation of Creation

Amsterdam, 1656

Nude in a garden of students, drugged
By a trick god, some Adam
Arranged on a table is muscle,
His eyes hooked on no Eve.
He's anchored by the head, a planet
Too dumb to break earth's orbit.
Where does his unhappiness lodge?
Dr. Deyman measures by string the skull.
Restricted to privacy of half a sheet,
The feet arc toward the ceiling.
The last and dimmest emanation,
This blossom of bruise, this body
Tests sterile dressings, dirt and rain.
Drugged in a garden of gods, students
Of tricks, some Adam arranged on a table
Is muscle to the thugs who'd beat him to atoms
If they could to know the body.

The Rest of the Year

His robes absolutely
Astonished you—
Whether you saw them in clouds
Scudding across the Rosh Hashanah sky
Or heard them swaying
In *Avenu Malkeinu*, Our Father Our King

By the time the Savior
has finished His excavations and soothed you
with the honey-salve and balm
of regal melodies, you're empty
but renewed, ready
to tumble from the altar.
The rest of the year,
plenty of time to sin
again, in small, delectable ways,
with your tongue, and if that doesn't
please, with your head.
Sinning, a collector's art.
You learn quickly to distinguish
the common from the rare,
you're alert in a dull place
for what others call a lucky find.
Before long your collection's good as gold,
and you know just how much to show off.
Then one day, late in the year,
you're whistling
your way home, kicking
an imaginary can down the field
a sidewalk makes, when suddenly

a bully grabs your neck
from behind. His breath
alone bruises you, his voice crushes
the petals of your ears.
You'd like to steal
a good look at the face,
but you know he'd have to burn
the memory out of you.
There's only one way out,
so you pay out the priceless card
no one but he would have believed
you carried casually in your pocket
like a private sin
the confession of which wins you
life, another year.

Survivors

Late one afternoon
After the children have stormed home,
In a schoolyard they gather.

One finds a ball
And lobs it to another,
Who shies it to a third,
And so on, the ball cuts
From hand to surprised hand,
A cheap ball, a pinky. Peel back
The skin of a kid's arm, what
You see's the color
Of this hollow rubber
Screaming across the yard.

No T-shirt to commemorate this reunion,
No program of names, dates and countries
Of birth, causes and places of death,
In the square, in the shower, before the eyes
Of a fruit vendor who, finally, looked away.
No bent spoon, no wig, no wheel,
No memorabilia of any kind on display.

If there must be flags, let them be the flags
Their faces have become, faded, thin,
Hanging in folds the way flags fly in no wind.

Yiddish Poets in America

The sky above us was silent and empty,
The earth below, silent, empty,
Our pockets were empty,
And our hands, empty, failed to fly.

We heard villages lock their gates,
We heard our language burn in a great fire,
And we urged it, the fire, to take
The tongue of our despair.

From yellow hearts we rescued no poems.
Nor can we purchase poems from the dead
Among whom we live in suburban verses.

Holocaust Day

Why cease our mourning?
So what if years have passed, if years
Are slabs on which condos have been built
And we've moved in.
The distance between us
And the immeasurable is no more
Than the distance between two rooms, even
If the wall is a heaving ocean.
When the coffee in our cup's disturbed,
We believe a bone in a mound of bones
A continent away has shifted
To trigger this local tremor.
When we're moved to kiss a stranger
On the street, we feel true
To a young couple long ago interrupted.
Our neighbors never can be just neighbors.
We embrace them like family:
They will betray us to the dogs
That roam the neighborhood,
The gentlemen who read our meters,
The flag snapping on Independence Day.
Like saplings planted in barren yards,
Our lamentations will mature
Long after we have crumbled.

The Rabbi's Wife

Where do you think
I go when you pray?
Do you believe
I am transported
to some heavenly garden?
I am a small woman.
I lift the child
when your wailing
frightens her.
We walk the road
away from here, stop
at a neighbor's fence
to touch the horse.
One day, when you are under
the shawl, they'll burn,
those cherished books
heaped in the study,
and you'll turn to me.
I'm another language.
Through the kitchen
window I watch
our daughter shrink
into the woods. What calls her? I
make do with what's here,
the stricken silence
now that you have fled
in search of God.

My People

My people drag a dead leg wherever they go.
They are like the horse pulling a cart
with a broken wheel.

My people, architects of an argument with God.
So many rooms, can't live in them all.
A room with a wall of salt,
a room stuffed with hair.

One of my people extends his hand
like a violin to a dark cloud.
Another goes with cows, grazes where they graze,
lies among them, stares with large, mute eyes
when a human figure approaches.

Someone should tell them the war is over.
Someone should steer them toward the grave sun.

The Jewish Angel

It doesn't answer to a Polish name
though it was once Polish, it isn't the light
going up like smoke to graze the ceiling,
it doesn't live for a cold bowl of borscht
with an island of sour cream floating on top,
it doesn't die each time it hears a sad violin.

The Jewish angel—it may be two angels,
two brothers, a farmer and a hunter,
a left arm and a right arm—this is my angel
as much as it is yours, it makes each of us
a little Jewish, each of us wander a little
from moon to moon, state to state,
it makes one of us crazy with coffee,
one of us drunk on tea.

I'm building my house out of old paperbacks,
westerns for the den, mysteries for the kitchen,
I'm saving the psalms until I've lived like David,
escaped to the woods, recruited the local birds
to my army, returned in a helmet of woven palmetto leaves
to claim my kingdom and God's, I'm polishing the
    candlesticks
and propping the window open, winter and spring, day
    and night,
for the wind.

Rabbi in the Garden

He hears insects ticking,
Tests burrs and thorns.
They remind him of his mother's armpit
Before she'd shave.

This year the tomatoes failed;
The tomatoes and peppers failed;
The tomatoes, peppers and berries—
Who has time to tend a garden?
He likes the wreckage of stalks.

A shrill silence, late
Afternoon, the children off with friends.
He bends to observe a bee.
For a moment he becomes the bee, taking
Off, lightly touching down.

He would like to touch his wife,
Lying together on the even grass.
Here they could move as if there were no Torah
Between them, two shadows
Spilled on the ground, a shallow pool of joy.

The Rabbi Who Does Not Observe

Practice is not his style,
But without practice, without
The regular deposit
Of glad coins into charity's mouth
And prayer at the time
Of defecation, without positioning
The straw so a wracked woman
Can suck a few beads of juice
Into her cavernous body
Or washing the corpse,
Without daily wrapping
Phylacteries and kissing
With fingertips the law
Hammered on the doorpost,
The law of walking, wheeling,
Sitting, the law to which
The tongue must submit, keep
It from wagging, law of linen,
Law of wool—without
Practice what is he
But a moth flicking
At a window, a page
Of *The Book of Splendor*.

The Eve of *Rosh Hashanah*, 500 Years after the Inquisition

My headache is a house
Of old newspapers, torn
Envelopes, threads, buttons
Gnawed dolls strewn
Everywhere, and on the stove
One burner lit. Why did I kiss
The road that led here?

My heartache is in the yard,
A red spruce, just another
Summer flourish.
But when the grass slows
And the glory of maple
And oak fades, the spruce alone
Retains its green poise
Like the penitential poem
That has survived cold
Centuries and every fall
Ignites the fuse that burns
From my pew to medieval Spain.

My return is up the path of books.
I read about ladling
And bandaging and bathing,
Kind acts and conversions
Until my head aches and my heart
Aches, the lamp
Outside my window turned low,
Another book to read tomorrow.

Will we be visited this year
By sweetness, this year by sorrow?
Once we and the Torah
And Cordoba were one.
My prayer before sleep
Dissolves like honey in the cup of night,
And the dog, overfed,
Snores among its beheaded joys.

After the Ritual Purification

we return the body,
    a sack of earth from Israel
        tucked neatly behind the arm,

to the coffin. Finished, we agree
    upon a pancake house.
        By the time hot plates arrive,

we're boating with Max
    and his father
        past a nudist camp.

The engine cut, father and son
    drift by families
        twinkling in the sun.

Let go, father says
    to the child squeezing
        his hand, you must

let go, says the suddenly ashen
    man as he plunges into the river.
        That's when I woke, Max tells us.

The dream wed
    my young father to father dying once again.
        He dips into a pool of syrup

a wedge of pancake.
 Waiting for a bus, I ease into my offering,
  in a dead neighborhood,

I see a woman walking
 who so stirs me
  I trail in her wake, hoping

for something sweet.
 When I am near, she spins
  and stuns me with a figure

I agree to pay.
 In a stranger's yard, behind a hedge,
  her bony body surprisingly soft,

she spoils me, then departs.
 This in Jerusalem,
  a few miles from the Temple Mount.

Smoke of sausage and cigarettes,
 and we go on recalling
  bodies beheld, bathed,

bruised, the buttocks
 of a man with whom we prayed
  on Yom Kippur, the name

we snipped from his toe.

Noah's Death Mask

Once this mask hid a face.
Now it is a face, a tranquil expression
Of one who has lived four thousand years listening to rain.
So much loneliness converges on the nose, its nostrils flare,
    wide to inhale
The last dust of the first kingdom, the blood-sweet scent of
    a world
That will not accompany him through water.
The cheeks, puffed like twin burial mounds
In a landscape that greens and reddens beyond them,
Nudge the ears as if to say,
Listen, the rain has stopped.

David's Body

While still turning in his mother's womb
    He recited a poem
He dreamed the day of death
    And chanted a poem
And like a dancer he whirled
    Before the ark of the Lord
His robes flung open
    His amber body exposed
    To slave-girls and the Lord
Verses to charm the Lord
    To make of human speech
A vessel worthy of the bowels
    Of a Moabite soldier,
    The burning livers of 7,000 Aramean charioteers
His verses a shield
    Against the Angel of Death
    Who guards the gate
    Through which he must pass into Jerusalem
Arameans Moabites Philistines Amalekites
    He could conquer
    But not the fear of perishing
So the King decreed, while still snug
    In his mother's womb
    Praise of Adonai my mouth shall speak
And let all flesh bless His holy name forever and ever
    And let the flesh of my words
    Be worthy of the lips of slave-girls

Tzimtzum: Contraction

The contractions
       have come
too soon   You are sentenced

      to bed   in the country house

During the tedious hours
your sons scrap   your husband courts
an imaginary lover   you summon the living

mothers: Hagar
               of the bitter smile
         Sarah
              whose laughter lies
         Rebecca
              who outwits men
        Leah Rachel
              phantom beauties

In such company you lie
opposed to
gravity that would steal
the new one   prematurely

Who brushes   your hair
who prepares   grains
who rubs   the mirror clear
        these attendants

And on the Sabbath
your men   like an Austrian forest
close around you   tall dark green

You sing   *n'sh*   *n'sham*   *n'shama*

till the eyes close

Come, now, new one
ride the waters
into your mother's arms
fill these woods with a cry

The Knot

It nearly killed me. I watched
    A stranger enter your mother
To free you, stunned by the sudden
    Pressure and release
Into the hands of a man who lay
    You under a lamp to pink up.
When, finally, in my arms
    You wailed, I learned
The cause of our distress:
    A knot in the cord, delivered
After you, scout, already good
    At a practical art
Worthy of a badge
    I'd proudly sew to the sleeve
Of a cotton jumper
    If badges were awarded to one-day-olds.

Now we seek other signs of intelligence.
    Will you fly or fall, sail
Or walk, hunt or lecture on knotty
    Problems of the heart?
She rocks, your mother,
    In a dark room, entranced
By your strong suck, proof
    Of the knot
Survived, not undone.

Witnesses

The stones underfoot, the brown-and-white horse
        at the fence,
The man at the broken water line, mud smeared
        over his plastic pants,
The secretary with a Bible underneath bills
        in her desk,
The dollar I leave for a tip, the ocean
        before which I stand,
The door through which I return home and flee,
The hair that grows while I sleep and work and love,
The hand I guide, hand with a will of its own,
The bee that flies from gutter to peach tree
        to gutter to screened window.

When called upon, the willow
        reports how I wasted my childhood,
The desk how I ruined my thirties
        composing obituaries, lies,
The charity box, how I push pathetic coins through its slot,
The shirts how infrequently I perspire,
The winds how rarely I raise my voice.

Whether I bow down or rise up, they are present,
        measuring the length of my stride, the speed
Of my mind, the arc of my pitch, the witnesses
        and the witness above all, Gabriel,
My infant son daily becoming more human.

Making Cain

It begins with terror, Adam

>Stripped of all joy, turns back
>For a last look—

>He's discovered the vault
>Of memory and it's empty—

But he can't make out anything distinct
Through the screen of fire

>Which, from such distance, is how
>The crossed swords appear

So he plunges into Eve, believing
He can rid himself of himself

Fool, Eve thinks, thrown
To the ground, by this

>He multiplies
>The cost of expulsion

Bless Us with Peace, Angels of Peace

The window's curtain drawn back,
Six panes of nightfall
Reflect wan faces that recall
The week and what it sorely lacked:

Humor, cash, good health.
Candlelight cannot cure all ills,
Nor can wine, a few drops of which spill
From the uplifted cup like excessive wealth.

But by the prayer with which we unveil
The braided breads, risen
Like our pride in being chosen
To receive Shabbat, our spirits heal.

Stuffed on *hallot*, our double portion,
We ease into the next course of fortune.

The Rabbi's Sabbatical

First he let one Sabbath pass, then another
Sampling uninhabited wind
Rather than the spirit he knew
Candlelight casts in the room.

In November, the fire that took a neighbor's barn
Pleased him, and he praised
His daughter who seduces with her art.

The woman he loves
Baked bread and consoled herself
When he was gone on one of the long walks
From which he'd return
Exhilarated, happier even than when he departed.

Like the Hebrews between a tyrant and the Law,
He rose each dawn, no hewn stone to lug.

He sang psalms, when he resumed
His duties, with the vigor of a renewed man,
His flesh bathed in black water under an apricot sun.

Two and One

Two roses I gave the therapist,
One for my thorny soul, one for hers.
Two answers to a step-daughter,
One in the hollow voice of her father.
Two days with an old friend,
One to recover the past,
One to recover from the past.
But I turn to one God only
When I lie down and rise up,
One God at the end of a day
When I empty the pockets,
And at dawn when I fill them again.

A proverb I recalled for my father
The day he confessed he was broke:
Rich man and poor man meet;
The Lord made them both;
He listened patiently.
Two gifts for the bride,
One of this world, one of the world to come.
But I labor to repair one world only
When I walk by the way.

Two coins for the beggar,
Two loaves for the Sabbath
Which ends when three stars open
In the Saturday night sky.
Two parents, neither one on this earth.
Two hands, one with which to give,
One with which to take away.
Two ears with which to hear, O Israel,
The Lord our God, the Lord is One.

Tekiah Gedolah

"Here are the firestone and the wood;
But where is the sheep for the burnt offering?"
That's the last we hear from the boy.
Abraham binds him, lays him out, picks up
The steel to slay him.
His life, apparently, meant
Less to his father, who, after all, had a reputation
For betraying kin, than pleasing God.
Abraham's hand was stayed, the kid
Spared. In his place, a ram
Caught in a thicket by its horns.
That's what we gather, once a year, to hear,
Not the story followed by the sermon that implores us to return,
But one of those horns, *tekiah, teruah, tekiah,*
Tekiah gedolah, enduring blast
That empties the lungs, Isaac's
Cry, his tongue
Cut out by our scribes
Lest he turn us away from this tribe,
At the moment of the testing,
With a description of the savage face of faith.

Notes

Tekiah (Hebrew: pronounced teh-key-'ah: def. blast, blowing of horn) The term *tekiah* refers to a sound made on the shofar, the ram's horn. One of the oldest Jewish symbols, the shofar is most strongly associated with Rosh Hashanah, the Jewish New Year. Blown annually on this holiday, the shofar recalls the story of the binding of Isaac, an event culminating in the sacrifice of a ram, hence the source of the horn. The sound also recalls the giving of the Ten Commandments, a revelation that was preceded by loud shofar blasts, and anticipates the messianic redemption. Finally, the shofar is an entreaty to Jewish worshipers to repent. The Baal Shem Tov suggests that the shofar teaches that repentance must come from the depths of the soul: "There are many halls in the king's palace, and intricate keys to all the doors, but the ax is stronger than all of these. The master key [to God's house] is the broken heart." The sound of the shofar suggests the wailing of that broken heart.

"The Good Jew": This poem is based on *The Protocols of the Elders of Zion*, a well-known forgery, published by the Russian secret police, purporting to document the alleged Zionist plan to take over the world.

"Ofra Haza": Haza's family was, in fact, not airlifted to Israel as part of the legendary rescue of Yemenite Jews known as Operation Magic Carpet. Her family emigrated on foot from Yemen to Israel.

"Prayer for the Bride": This poem is dedicated to Laurie Chess to whom thanks are also due for suggesting the book's title.

"The Week": *Tefillin* are the phylacteries strapped to the arm and head by observant Jews as part of the morning prayer ritual.

"From the Introduction to the New Jewish Prayerbook": *Shekinah*, King of Kings, and *Ayn Sof* are terms used in reference to God.

"Harvest Booth": During Sukkot, a harvest festival, also known as Tabernacles or the Feast of Booths, Jews build a hut (sukkah), a temporary structure usually constructed of four walls with a roof of tree branches. For the duration of the week-long holiday, meals are eaten in the sukkah. Some Jews also practice the custom of inviting symbolic guests, the patriarchs and matriarchs of the Jewish people, to join them in the sukkah. *Lulav* is "palm branch"; *etrog* means "citron."

"After the Ritual Purification": According to Jewish tradition, the bodies of the deceased are prepared for burial in a simple and dignified manner by members of a *chevra kadisha*, a holy burial society. This poem is dedicated to Rabbi Shmuel Birnham.

"*Tzimtzum*: Contraction": In his book *Innerspace* Rabbi Aryeh Kaplan writes, "The word *Tzimtzum* means 'constriction' [or contraction], and refers to the process by which God 'withdrew' His light in order to create the universe." *N'shama* is one of three Hebrew terms for soul. This poem is dedicated to Marc Rudow and Debi Miles.

Acknowledgments

The author and publisher gratefully acknowledge the following publications in which these poems first appeared, often in different form.

American Literary Review: "Making Cain," "The Rabbi's Hand"
American Voice: "Baby Boomer," "The Week," "The Rabbi's Wife"
Asheville Poetry Review: "After the Ritual Purification," "The Rabbi Disturbed," "The Rabbi Masturbates"
College English: "The Rest of the Year"
Confrontations: "David's Body"
Hubbub: "Rabbi in the Garden"
Louisiana Literature: "The Eve of Rosh Hashanah, 500 Years after the Inquisition," "Holocaust Day"
Massachusetts Review: "Survivors"
New Virginia Review: "Guardians: Variations on a Theme from Psalm 34"
North Carolina Humanities: "Trip to the Museum," "The Rabbi's Sabbatical"
Onthebus: "The Good Jew," "My People"
Orim: A Jewish Journal at Yale: "The Skin That Shelters," "Noah's Death Mask"
Ploughshares: "*Tzimtzum*: Contraction"
Poetry: "Growing Up in a Jewish Neighborhood," "At the Rabbi's Study Group"
Poetry East: "Rabbi qua Mystic"
The Reaper: "With the Blast of the Ram's Horn"
Shenandoah: "From the Introduction to the New Revised Prayer Book"
Shirim: "The Jewish Angel"
The Sun: "Prayer for the Bride"
Tampa Review: "The Tenth Emanation of Creation," "Nothing but Pleasure"
Tikkun: "The Wrestler," "That's How It Is"

I would like to thank the Virginia Center for the Creative Arts for four fellowships and the University of North Carolina at Asheville for reassigned time during which many of these poems were written.

Special thanks also to Robin Behn, Donald Morrill, and Sidney Wade for their invaluable assistance.

Richard Chess is an associate professor of literature and language at the University of North Carolina at Asheville. His poems have been anthologized in *Telling and Remembering: A Century of American Jewish Poetry* as well as in other anthologies. His work appears frequently in *Tampa Review*, the *Forward*, *Slate*, *Prairie Schooner*, and other journals. He directs the Center for Jewish Studies at UNCA as well as UNCA's undergraduate program in creative writing.

www.ingramcontent.com/pod-product-compliance
Lightning Source LLC
Chambersburg PA
CBHW030309100526
44590CB00012B/576